THE FROZEN SOLACE

THE WHINE OF COMPASSION IN THE TIMBERLAND

PRANEETHA CHOWDARY

To all my amazing readers who did not lose their innocence and madness yet!

Contents

Contents

Foreword

What could be a joy in itself to explore uncertainty which is described beautifully in various forms of adjectives that one has to feel in life either by choice or fate; The book "The Frozen Solace -The Whine of Compassion in the Timberland" holds the compression of infinite love, adaptation, and sensation besides soreness in the life of a woman. The author through her poetic words wring out her deep down thoughts as a girl, emplace involvement for unusual events and the way she holds the grip of life and relationship by spreading the charm.

The inbuilt delicacy - the robustness, you are just not a creature to authorise someone to lead you, so do not let inner bashfulness takeover the blight. Each word picked by the author hits you hard to recall your memory of deep down wounds that starts growing as a new pain giving life to a new strain. The moments to cherish for feel in love which is unseen but the fragrance is spread across throughout the life and probably that's the beautiful beginning and like how beautiful a person assumes to be treated with all the love and care she deserves. Flaunt like the clouds that hide the sun behind and dance on the rainbow with all your colours within.

-Syed Rizwan

Author of 'Wings to fly to another world.'

Preface

And one fine day, writing became my morning sunshine and twilight moonlight.

As a reader, you either be amazed at the time of representations by a writer or you be a part of boring letters. The choice lies within an inch mood of this relativity. You float on the curls of smoothness pushing the boundaries between you and the writer. The absolute possibility is within your walking distance from the very beginning of virtue. A reader laughs at the expressions of the writer.

Acknowledgements

My endless gratitude to the divine musical energy of the universe and the language of artistic expressions and emotions conveying the feelings for and from all the living things.

I'm much obliged to my mother who had been a warm home of my heart. Thanks a bunch to all my friends who had been a great support throughout my journey of writing.

I would also like to express my special thanks to my colleagues and the management of Gopalan College, for their guidance and encouragement in the evolution of my ideas.

Prologue

Take your body into the nature

And sing the depressing conception!

HELLO LITERARY CRITICS!

The space between us be filled with mind's eye.

HAPPY READING.

1. Fitful

We are all broken!
Finding a way to escape into
An elastic world which wouldn't
Defame your perceptiveness
And bottled-up emotions;
You've deceived yourself into an
Agreement on a new way of delighting
The shrewdness which could victimize you.

2. Sanity

Positivity is a popular fooling idea
Restricting a persona to behave in an
Actuality without turning over the things.
The human mind is conditioned to act like
A great intelligence amongst ridiculous
Intellectually disabled dumb egregious
Deeds causing ache for maleficent.

3. Vigor

I am mademoiselle with stains of
Bravery and throbbed chasteness,
Uncovering fondness to crown with
Classic rock untamed lyrics all sailing
Towards warmness of the surface;
Yet drowning in gore of sensing
The squishy patter of tiny feet.

4. Adore

And we all knew that no quantity of richness
Of an individual can make your day unique!
Why are we still blind-eyed selves with no real love and bonding?
If money could make you shine with gold:
What are you without gold and glories?
Aren't we just fooled into the competition
Of being wealthy however suffocated we are?
Why are we bad at breathing compassion?
This time let's not forget to love and only
To love to live rather than just a few valid days!!

5. Communion

And there I heard the harmony,
That clasped the phenomenon
Of finding friendship with a
Bird not longing for a firm place!
Constructing an indefinite nest for
A seasoned tang added a ray of
Shadow: there I grasped solidity!

6. Sing

Believe in your experience!
You're not a sheep to obey;
Don't feel the way your old-timers felt
You are here to live your life
Not to live as theirs first!
Appreciate yourself for being
A free spirit of one's own!
It's wonderful to feel everything:
Express your condolence to those
Who humiliates your own emotions.
Let not their idiotic words harm you!
You are as beautiful as a cloud,
Who holds on to the sprouts:
Take your body into the nature
And sing the depressing conception.

7. Ordain Off

Conditioning has never been helpful!
You cannot condition a plant,
To grow high and perpendicular;
Fairly, you can only lay assistance:
To grow in an assumed path!
The plant decides whether to
Bloom glorious flowers or not;
Here, you can only speculate
But not authorize the life!

8. Put On

To pretend to be alive while you're
Dead inside is the greatest misery of all!
You can neither take breathe nor neglect it
That state where your breath struck is
The day you need to realise about losing yourself.
The poisonous love which was once sweet
Had killed you this day for your emotions;
You live not for yourself but rather for their
Pleasure to fulfil themselves and their soul.
This world doesn't deserve you for
You are here only to survive and kill yourself
Each day by being one among frauds!

9. Blush

I soften up like thee
Of velvety compassion!
The cuddling therapy from
Glittering bronzy crunches
Of an aromatic full moon:
To the rhythm of cravings;
Wings of gratification trusting
Thy glances glowed up to the sky.

10. Embracing Feminity

Pseudo-intellectuals stand for violating
The excitement of untamed eroticism.
Not-too-distant future is overhanging
On the bottom lip thirsting for a loud slurp
Of elixir procuring gladness of move
Caught up in rounds of ideal lovemaking;
Thriving under the shadow of concealed
Physique, I set my heart on shades of
Lavender fashioned into cutis about
Entwined in the bosom of womanhood.

11. Loiter

A ride on simplicity with a wind
Of heaven dancing alongside,
I experienced surprising happiness
from brief moments of longing!

12. Peel off

My heart aches for the arrow-like
Questions and uncertainties from him!
I, being unnoticed by the love of my day
Had been into the unconscious urge to
Fall asleep on the path of least misgivings.
The fault of my words which can never be
Taken back left me with the heaviness that
None can take away from my temperament!
Helpless I am to the point of being impotent
And here I roll out the tears and breathe out!

13. Honor

And then our eyes met Like ocean waves of wish;
Inclining towards the beginning
Of a new phase of prosperity!
Embracing the differences by
Celebrating the similitude of dreams:
We had begun painting abstract
Flowers and petals of tenderness!

14. Unique

The more you get rotten for a new energy
The less you dislike the pungent smell;
New life out of a decomposed body
Is the exotic contentment with melody!

15. Who

That was the day when I questioned
The universe who would heal me?
Who would take my pain away?
Who would make me feel better?
Who would wipe my tears away?
Who would care about my tears?
Who would be with me till the last day?
Who would understand me?
Who wouldn't judge me for what I'm?
Who would listen to me just the way fairies listen to the most beautiful women?

16. Charm

It was overwhelming for the sky
To shadow a lightning cloud!
As the goddess nut walked to
Silhouette is another unfamiliar cloud
Flowers roared to the raising sparkles;
And that was heaven and arduous
For they name it phenomenal!!

17. Perceive

You don't have to acquit yourself all the time
To be the so-called best and good
Amongst allowed pains and pleasures.
You are holed up in stagnant situations
Humans aren't machines to behave in
A proportional way of not being in a
Motive state that exists in imperial Valley;

18. Distant

Staying miles away from you;
Feeling the blessings of your words
Smiling and weeping to the memories:
I feel that warmth of your love and care!

19. Blight

One decaying fruit is reasonable to make a
Bunch of fruits terrible of surviving: so as the
Love from a cunning person is, you assume
That it makes you rejuvenate inevitably
You fall in despair when you understand that
The very thing is worsening the life by taking
Away the fundamental posture of being loved!

20. Uncertanity

As a child, we grew up believing in lies
That were warned of not doing something wrong.
As a fact of life, we all followed it losing our
Strength by repressing the ability to prosper.
The more you hold a bud from blossoming,
The more it lets out the life by wringing the neck of its essence.

21. Fool

Dear heartless society,
I know I was one among you,
I believed in your lies and assumptions;
I was a fool fooled by fools!

22. You

My heart puffed up when my eyes clasped you!
My legs rode in ballads while residing in your composure.
And all my joy is to feel life spring from the flower fountain
That keeps filling all the paths of my nerves.

23. Cherish

I'm greatly thankful to you for holding
My emotions that warm up the glittering stars.
Travel in a sea of unbridled imagination by
A boat of my words to experience
The lost beauty of tenderness!

24. Affliction

Pain lives longer than a life!
Pain isn't just for the body to heal by itself.
It is to the sensitive soul of innocence
Which knows no bounds of survival;
An unusual flow of dead mood swings warned
The child half-cut feathers of compassion.
Vulgar words greeted with an extreme stay of
Gentleness and a bow for family reasons;
Pockets filled up with grief of chasing doubts
Sorrowful hidden breeze hurried to bring peace by force.

25. Enact

Soon after you find out all the
Things that can go wrong,
Your life becomes less about living
And more about surviving by waiting
For the right things to germinate in lush bliss.

26. Awe

I wandered from one plight to another
In search of well-being and no hostage;
I was distressed that the human race could tear
Apart from my veins for hidden themes of life.
They were all cramped in the spectacular view
Of luxuriousness as a yield to unexpressed
Disconsolation: to deny resistance.
Possessed of deploying affinities with
All and sundry to the heebie-jeebies;

27. Piety

If a male could fool you with words
Such as character and purity- be a dog
And fool yourself: for letting him ask you!
When a woman speaks of these - be a lioness
Shut her mouth with razor-sharper looks!
That's how you survive in a world of fools!

28. Malice

Your misery is candy-coated;
It is gliding solely by warping you to burn!
You've invited the conspiracy to unconcern.
You as a plant green-eyed: of the flower
Growing on the other plant of prosperity.
And you cannot grow a flower out of enmity.
The universe, pollination happens to be life
So as you and I are going to reap
Remember that one does not become
Enlightened by choosing to be in the dark!

29. Sense

Where being fat is deemed to be disgraceful
I rose as a lotus out of a muddy pond;
Fearless towards the polluted huffing
I smiled with the pinkish cheeks to exhibit
The untamed faultlessness in being fluffy!
While the flowers shimmered in colours,
I sparkled like a natural sensation.

30. Unrest

And then I lost my strength in words!!
That was the moment I felt to leave
This world as soon as possible,
Where I was once the one who
Endorsed people to come out of despair.
Questioning them or myself didn't take
My worries away: I'm getting mad!
Mad about the things that I never change!
What am I going to survive for?

31. Desire

I desire and dream
A need beyond the cracked hills!

Your lust _______
My affection _______

Huddled profound into the abbey,
On the grounds of sense and despair!

I gush and bloom as a fire
To dust off the bench of darkness.

32. Espy

Sleepless night longing to see the
Amazed beauty bud shooting at
My wild enthusiasm for growing life;
Plump prettiness of young floret
Air kissing the burden of a generation
To relieve the overcrowded heart.
Seeking shelter from your love
I aspire to breathe compassion!

33. Oh my Art!

If you can love my art indefinitely,
my love for you doesn't seem any harder than flakes.
Ah, oh the Golden Gate is stuffed with cheese and fresh apples.
And inside! The sweetest manners of oranges and blue eyes
Collapsed while spectacles fell in love with toothpicks.
Red Wine overflowing out of the paper boat cleansed
The brown bench making it easily available for the new couple,
flies fencing the area twittered sleepily in the ears of evil.

34. Insight

Mistaken as the sign of destruction!
Preserving the jar of inhumane cherries
To cherish the forgotten utility of gleam:
The sphere prospering bit of all right,
To provide a place of healing than
Establishing the land of mercilessness:
The sweet smell of human values flourished
Under the gifted roof of self-healing.
The lovely state of cheerfulness defeated
The stupidity of mechanical arrogance
Empathy stood greater than a personage.

35. Ease

Relax, that's the real little wine of art!
Neither you've to get worried about
The moon for its darkest of shades:
Nor do: you've to worry about, how I share
My uniqueness in this world is a ray of
Sunshine that dares to demolish reductions.

Printed by Libri Plureos GmbH in Hamburg, Germany